Ladybug

Horned Beetle

Stinkbug

Stick Bug

This book is dedicated to my son, Jason, because of his appreciation for the small things in life, including bugs.

這本書要獻給我的兒子——Jason，因為他總能去欣賞生活中的微小事物，包括小蟲子。

Stinky's Funny Scent

丁奇的怪味道

Stinky the stinkbug finds a big, red *strawberry. He sees Lily the ladybug sitting on a *daisy.

"This *berry is too big for me. Maybe I can share my berry with Lily."

Stinky lands beside Lily.

"Want to share my berry, Lily?" he asks.

"Sure! Mmmm. It's sweet!"

Stinky is so happy that his funny scent *gets out.

Lily *coughs and covers her nose.

6

"Ugh! What's that smell?"

"It's me," Stinky says. "I'm sorry, Lily."

"Oh no!" Lily cries. "Sorry, Stinky. I'm not hungry any more." She flies away.

Stinky feels sad.

"It's no fun being lonely," he says.

He sees Fleet the fly playing "*kick the *seed" with Macy the mantis. "I can't share my berry, but maybe I can join the game."

11

Macy kicks a grass seed high into the air.

"I'll get it!" Stinky cries.

He *bounces the seed high in the air. He's so happy
that he lets his funny scent out.

"Ugh! What's that smell?" Fleet and Macy ask.

14

"Sorry! It's me," Stinky says. "My funny scent is out."

"You're a good player, Stinky," Macy says. "But—"

"Your scent makes my eyes *water," Fleet says.

"I'll just watch you play then," Stinky says sadly.

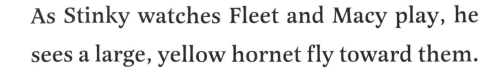

As Stinky watches Fleet and Macy play, he sees a large, yellow hornet fly toward them.

"Run, Fleet! Run, Macy!" Stinky cries. "It's Buzzer the hornet. She looks *mad!"

Fleet flies away, but Macy *trips.

"You're too close to my nest!" Buzzer *warns.

She *aims her *stinger at Macy.

Stinky points his *shell at Buzzer. A stinky smell covers the hornet.

"Yuck!" Buzzer cries.

She *rubs her face, then flies back to her nest.

"Wow!" Macy cries. "Your funny scent saved me!"
"Come and play!" Fleet says. "We think your scent is great!"

生_{ㄕㄥ}字_{ㄗˋ}表_{ㄅㄧㄠˇ}

funny [ˋfʌnɪ] adj. 怪_{ㄍㄨㄞˋ}異_{ㄧˋ}的_{ㄉㄜ˙}

scent [sɛnt] n. 氣_{ㄑㄧˋ}味_{ㄨㄟˋ}

p.2

strawberry [ˋstrɔ͵bɛrɪ] n. 草_{ㄘㄠˇ}莓_{ㄇㄟˊ}

daisy [ˋdezɪ] n. 雛_{ㄔㄨˊ}菊_{ㄐㄩˊ}

p.3

berry [ˋbɛrɪ] n. 莓_{ㄇㄟˊ}果_{ㄍㄨㄛˇ}

p.6

get out　　散_{ㄙㄢˋ}發_{ㄈㄚ}

cough [kɔf] v. 咳_{ㄎㄜˊ}嗽_{ㄙㄡˋ}

p.11

kick [kɪk] v. 踢_{ㄊㄧ}

seed [sid] n. 種_{ㄓㄨㄥˇ}子_{ㄗˇ}

26

adj.=形ㄒㄧㄥˊ容ㄖㄨㄥˊ詞ㄘˊ，n.=名ㄇㄧㄥˊ詞ㄘˊ，v.=動ㄉㄨㄥˋ詞ㄘˊ

丁ㄉㄧㄥ奇ㄑㄧˊ的ㄉㄜ怪ㄍㄨㄞˋ味ㄨㄟˋ道ㄉㄠˋ

臭ㄔㄡˋ蟲ㄔㄨㄥˊ丁ㄉㄧㄥ奇ㄑㄧˊ找ㄓㄠˇ到ㄉㄠˋ了ㄌㄜ一ㄧ顆ㄎㄜ又ㄧㄡˋ大ㄉㄚˋ又ㄧㄡˋ紅ㄏㄨㄥˊ的ㄉㄜ草ㄘㄠˇ莓ㄇㄟˊ。

他ㄊㄚ看ㄎㄢˋ到ㄉㄠˋ瓢ㄆㄧㄠˊ蟲ㄔㄨㄥˊ莉ㄌㄧˋ莉ㄌㄧˋ坐ㄗㄨㄛˋ在ㄗㄞˋ一ㄧ朵ㄉㄨㄛˇ雛ㄔㄨˊ菊ㄐㄩˊ上ㄕㄤˋ。

「這ㄓㄜˋ顆ㄎㄜ草ㄘㄠˇ莓ㄇㄟˊ太ㄊㄞˋ大ㄉㄚˋ了ㄌㄜ，我ㄨㄛˇ吃ㄔ不ㄅㄨˋ完ㄨㄢˊ，也ㄧㄝˇ許ㄒㄩˇ我ㄨㄛˇ
可ㄎㄜˇ以ㄧˇ跟ㄍㄣ莉ㄌㄧˋ莉ㄌㄧˋ一ㄧ起ㄑㄧˇ吃ㄔ。」

丁ㄉㄧㄥ奇ㄑㄧˊ飛ㄈㄟ到ㄉㄠˋ莉ㄌㄧˋ莉ㄌㄧˋ身ㄕㄣ旁ㄆㄤˊ。

他ㄊㄚ問ㄨㄣˋ:「莉ㄌㄧˋ莉ㄌㄧˋ，想ㄒㄧㄤˇ不ㄅㄨˋ想ㄒㄧㄤˇ跟ㄍㄣ我ㄨㄛˇ一ㄧ起ㄑㄧˇ吃ㄔ草ㄘㄠˇ莓ㄇㄟˊ啊ㄚ?」

「好ㄏㄠˇ啊ㄚ！嗯ㄣ……好ㄏㄠˇ甜ㄊㄧㄢˊ喔ㄛ！」

丁ㄉㄧㄥ奇ㄑㄧˊ太ㄊㄞˋ高ㄍㄠ興ㄒㄧㄥˋ了ㄌㄜ，一ㄧ不ㄅㄨˋ小ㄒㄧㄠˇ心ㄒㄧㄣ，身ㄕㄣ體ㄊㄧˇ就ㄐㄧㄡˋ發ㄈㄚ出ㄔㄨ

了怪味道。

莉莉一邊咳嗽，一邊掩住她的鼻子。

「噁！那是什麼味道啊？」

丁奇說：「是我。莉莉，真對不起！」

莉莉大叫：「不會吧？不好意思，丁奇，我一點都不餓了。」

說完她就飛走了。丁奇覺得有點難過。

「自己一個人一點也不好玩。」

他看到蒼蠅飛麗和螳螂莓西在玩「踢種子」的遊戲。

「我找不到人跟我一起吃草莓，但也許我可以跟她們一起玩遊戲。」

莓西把種子高高的踢到空中。

丁奇大叫：「我來接！」

他把種子彈到高空中。他玩得太開心了，一不小心，身上又散發出怪味道。

30

飛麗和莓西問：「噁！那是什麼味道啊？」

丁奇說：「不好意思，是我，我身上的怪味跑出來了。」

莓西說：「丁奇，你球踢得不錯，但是……」

飛麗接著說：「你的臭味嗆得我眼淚都流出來了。」

丁奇難過的說：「那我在旁邊看妳們玩好了。」

當丁奇在旁邊看著飛麗和莓西玩時，他看

到一隻大黃蜂朝他們飛過來。

丁奇大叫：「快跑呀，飛麗！跑呀，莓西！黃蜂芭茲來了，她看起來很生氣！」

飛麗飛走了，但是莓西卻跌倒了。

芭茲警告他們：「你們離我的蜂巢太近了！」她把她的刺對準莓西。

丁奇把他的甲殼對準芭茲；一瞬間，一股臭味圍繞著大黃蜂。

32

芭兹大叫：「好噁心！」

她抹了抹臉，然後就飛回她的巢穴。

莓西大叫：「哇！你的怪味道救了我一命！」

飛麗說：「一起來玩吧！我們覺得你的怪味道太棒了！」

搶救蟲蟲大作戰！
Bug Bingo!

故事裡的蟲蟲們被困在蜘蛛網上了！
小朋友，快來拯救牠們吧！

1 將第 43-44 頁的昆蟲圖片一個個剪下來，按照自己喜歡的順序，排列在下面的格子裡。

2 請聽 CD 的 Track 4，將被唸到的蟲蟲從格子上救出來。一次只能救一隻喔！

3 不管是直的、橫的或斜的，只要出現連續四個空格，就成為一條線。

4 當空格連成四條線，任務就完成囉！

5 你也可以將第 43-44 頁的昆蟲圖片和右頁的格子影印下來，邀請你的爸爸媽媽或好朋友一起來比賽，看誰先把蟲蟲救出來！

　　書中 stinkbug 就是俗稱的臭蟲、臭腥龜仔，牠們會有這樣的俗名，是因為許多臭蟲都會排放腥臭味的體液來趕走敵人。臭蟲的嘴巴像蚊子一樣，尖尖長長的像吸管，只能吸食液體；所以吃素的臭蟲會吸食樹液，吃葷的則吸食其他昆蟲的體液維生。

　　除了臭蟲之外，還有其他的動植物也會散發臭味喔！動物界中，最臭名昭彰的就是臭鼬了。牠會用特殊的臭味來警告敵

人不要攻擊牠：如果敵人靠得太近，臭鼬會低下身，豎起尾巴，用前爪跺地發出警告；如果敵人不聽警告，臭鼬便會轉過身作倒立狀，用惡臭的液體噴向敵人。而在植物界，高雄柴山上就有兩種植物開花時會發出臭味——密毛魔芋和台灣魔芋；它們散發臭味不是為了禦敵，而是為了吸引喜愛腐食的蠅類替它們傳粉。

關於作者

Kriss Erickson has been a freelance writer since 1981. She has published in the United States and in Australia and has over 300 published works. Kriss earned a Master's degree in Counseling in 2003 and holds a Master's level certificate of Spiritual Direction. She lives with her husband and son on a 3/4 acre wetland where she has created extensive gardens. Kriss is also a freelance artist in colored pencil and acrylic. She enjoys singing blues and contemporary music at local coffee shops.

Kriss Erickson 從 1981 年開始了自由作家的生活。她陸續在美國和澳洲發表著作，至今出版過的作品已超過 300 本。Kriss 在 2003 年取得心理諮商碩士的學位，並且擁有靈修指導碩士程度的結業證書。她和丈夫以及兒子住在四分之三英畝的濕地上，還在那裡打造了一個廣闊的花園。Kriss 同時也是一位自由藝術家，擅長使用色鉛筆和壓克力顏料來畫畫，而在當地的咖啡店哼唱藍調和現代音樂則是她的樂趣。

關於繪者

陽光，綠蔭，
花和青草味，
樹影和月光，蛙鳴。
童年的盛夏。

一個透明的玻璃瓶，瓶口用橡皮筋箍著紙蓋，上面扎有幾個氣孔，將裡面裝滿大大小小的、知名的或是不知名的蟲兒，然後安靜而好奇的看上好長一陣子，這是整個季節裡最興趣盎然的事情之一了。許多歲以後，複雜、莫名的東西多起來，心中不再有那個帶紙蓋的瓶子，不再關心、甚至不再靜心聆聽周圍的一切。

身為卡圖工作室的一份子，畫畫、做書，我們努力為孩子們製造著快樂，同樣也為自己尋找單純和美好。

親親自然 成就英語悅讀

台北市外語啟蒙教學發展學會理事長　　李宗玥

　　「故事」是每個孩子的夢工廠，成就孩子的豐富幻想，讓孩子的想像力無限伸展與飛翔，每個故事都在架構成長的快樂回憶，細數故事的數目，如同細數快樂。

　　「自然世界」是兒童生活經驗中，最真實與迷人的經驗。不起眼的毛毛蟲為什麼會變成一隻漂漂亮亮的蝴蝶？自然世界裡充滿了讓孩子忍不住驚喜的讚嘆，如同作者的孩子，琢磨於生活中的微小事物，一隻小蟲子也能成就一個大驚奇，從孩子的眼裡視察自然，會發現自然世界本身就是一個故事屋。

　　「語言」是迎向世界最萬能的鑰匙，它開啟每一扇快樂夢想的門；而每一扇門後，有著世界各個角落裡孩子的喜悅與幻想。有了語言的鑰匙，才有機會透視世界更多的快樂夢想，才有機會了解故事裡的昆蟲們，是如何相處互動的。

三民書局的「我的昆蟲朋友」系列，用「語言」的骨架，串連了「故事」與「自然世界」，搭起孩子閱讀的興趣與動機，讓「語言」(language) 與「知識」(knowledge) 不再毫無交集、枯燥乏味。就是這樣的書，會讓我們和孩子都感動。任何一種有目的的學習，在學習歷程中，都會有高低潮，我相信藉著「我的昆蟲朋友」系列中有趣的自然故事與好玩的學習活動，必然能逐步架構語言的樂趣與能力。

　　語言的學習，早就應擺脫制式語言文法架構，而走入孩子的真實生活裡。如果您也有同樣的想法，相信在「昆蟲朋友」的「自然世界」中，必能滿足您對孩子語言發展的夢想與期盼。

FUN心讀雙語叢書

BUG BUDDIES SERIES 我的昆蟲朋友系列

具基礎英文閱讀能力者（國小 4 ～ 6 年級適讀）

我有幾個昆蟲好朋友，各個都有自己奇怪的特性，讓他們有點煩惱；可是這樣的不同，卻帶給他們意想不到的驚奇與結果！

「我的昆蟲朋友」共有五個：

1. Bumpy's Crazy Tail　　邦皮的瘋狂尾巴
2. Fleet's Sticky Feet　　飛麗的黏腳丫
3. Stilt's Stick Problem　史提的大麻煩
4. Macy's Strange Snacks　莓西的怪點心
5. Stinky's Funny Scent　丁奇的怪味道

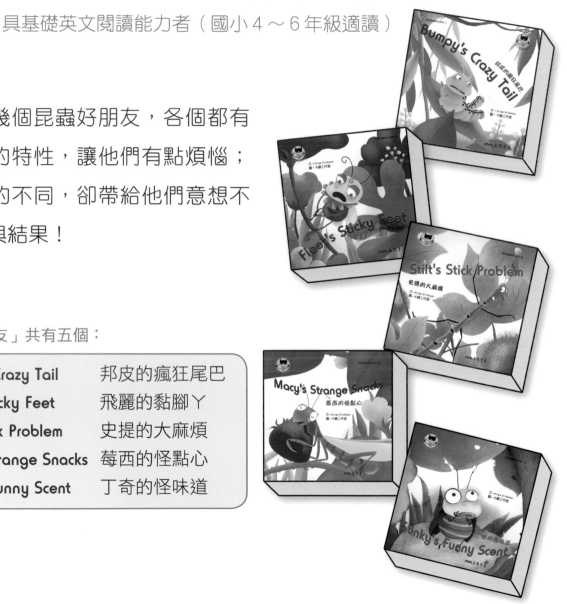

Stinky the stinkbug	Stinky the stinkbug	Stinky the stinkbug	Stinky the stinkbug
Fleet the fly	Lily the ladybug	Lily the ladybug	Lily the ladybug
Macy the mantis	Macy the mantis	Fleet the fly	Fleet the fly
Buzzer the hornet	Buzzer the hornet	Buzzer the hornet	Macy the mantis

國家圖書館出版品預行編目資料

Stinky's Funny Scent:丁奇的怪味道 / Kriss Erick-
son著;卡圖工作室繪;本局編輯部譯.－－初版一
刷.－－臺北市：三民，2006
　　面；　　公分.－－(Fun心讀雙語叢書.我的昆蟲
　　朋友系列)
中英對照
ISBN 957－14－4593－2　（精裝）

1. 英國語言－讀本

523.38　　　　　　　　　　　　　　95014826

© **Stinky's Funny Scent**
　　——丁奇的怪味道

著作人　　Kriss Erickson
繪　者　　卡圖工作室
譯　者　　本局編輯部
發行人　　劉振強
著作財
產權人　　三民書局股份有限公司
　　　　　臺北市復興北路386號
發行所　　三民書局股份有限公司
　　　　　地址／臺北市復興北路386號
　　　　　電話／(02)25006600
　　　　　郵撥／0009998－5
印刷所　　三民書局股份有限公司
門市部　　復北店／臺北市復興北路386號
　　　　　重南店／臺北市重慶南路一段61號
初版一刷　2006年8月
編　號　　S 806771
定　價　　新臺幣參佰元整
行政院新聞局登記證局版臺業字第○二○○號

有著作權·不准侵害

ISBN　957－14－4593－2　（精裝）

http://www.sanmin.com.tw　三民網路書店